RELIGION

by Desmond Painter
and John Shepherd

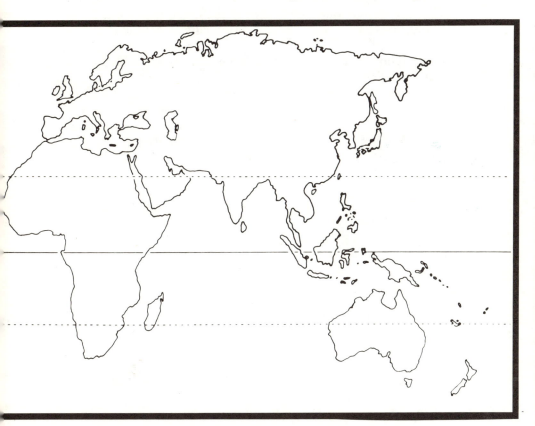

Greenhaven Press, Inc.

P.O. BOX 289009
SAN DIEGO, CA 92198-0009

The story of man and religion forms one of the most widespread and lasting themes in world history. Nobody has yet found a complete answer to such questions as: 'Why are we here in this world?'; 'Why should we behave as we do?'; and 'What happens when we die?' The search for answers to questions like these is the basis of religion. The answers given have led to the building of great systems of rules and huge organizations controlling much of the life of people throughout history. In this booklet we will look at the story of this search, at the different religions which have come out of it, and at their effects upon people throughout the world.

RELIGIOUS BELIEFS

Primitive Man

Little is known about the men of the Old Stone Age, but it is known that man was religious in prehistoric times. He believed in supernatural powers which influenced his life and in turn he tried to influence them. Nature played an important part in early man's way of life; a bad harvest could mean starvation and even death. Man worshipped certain aspects of nature — the sun, the rain, the sky and rivers were thought of as *gods*, supernatural beings which had to be influenced in order to ensure a good harvest (D1)*.

The gods were often shown in human or animal form in cave paintings and carvings. Often the gods were thought of as spirits living perhaps in a tree, a mountain, or a spring, and many stories (myths) came to be told about these early gods (D2).

Polytheism

Polytheism means a belief in many gods (rather than just one god). In ancient times, people who lived in places as far apart as India, Persia and Greece worshipped many different gods such as a god of the sky, one for thunder, a sun god, a god of the crops and so on. There are many similarities between the gods of different countries — for example, Zeus is very like the Indian sky god Dyaus. The Indian god Mitra is connected with the Persian sun god Mithras, who was later worshipped by the Romans as far west as the Roman province of Britain. Temples were often built to these various gods and gifts were offered to them so that in return man would get a good harvest or the right sort of weather.

Science

Because early religions were often concerned with the sowing and harvesting of crops, it was important to be able to work out the time of the year correctly. In this way some of man's mathematical and scientific achievements grew out of religion. The Aztec priests, for example, produced a complicated and accurate calendar, which shows they had a detailed knowledge of astronomy. (*Ancient America*)** The careful construction of many religious buildings such as the

*The reference (D) indicates the numbered documents at the end of this book

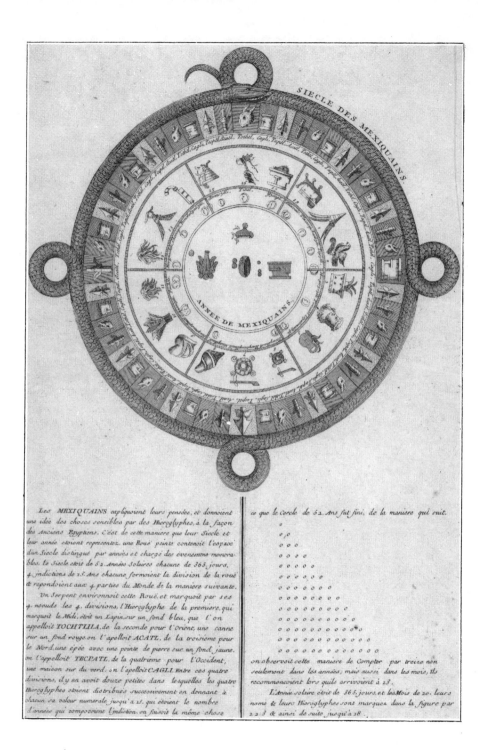

Aztec calendar, ancient Mexico

**Titles in brackets refer to other booklets in the Program   3

Paintings by South African Bushmen

Pyramids shows that their builders knew a lot about geometry. (*The Ancient Near East*) In some parts of the world (especially in China) attempts to find an 'elixir' to make people live longer led priests to study alchemy, out of which grew our modern sciences of chemistry and biology (D3).

Folk Religions

In many parts of the world, beliefs and practices similar to those of the old religions still exist. This kind of religion (sometimes called 'folk religion') is often mixed up with magic — the belief that mysterious forces can be controlled by spells and ceremonies. The 'wise men' of Siberia (*Chingis Khan and the Mongol Empire*), the 'witch doctors' of Africa (*Traditional Africa*) and the Red Indian 'medicine men' of North America all had much influence in their societies because they were thought to know the secrets of controlling these forces.

We can see many traces of these old religions. For example, Thursday is named after Thor, the Norse god of thunder. The use of

Zulu witch doctor, South Africa, 1900

holly as a decoration at Christmas is a reminder that our ancestors regarded evergreen trees as sacred, because they flourished and bore fruit in the middle of winter, when everything else was dead. Even the Christian festival of Christmas itself is connected with the celebration of the winter solstice, after which the days begin to lengthen again and bring promise of a new spring.

World Religions

Most folk religion is local, that is it is followed by one family, village or tribe. Other religions have been followed by large numbers of people and spread through many countries. We call these 'world religions' and the chart shows some facts about the six religions with the most followers.

RELIGION AND SOCIETY

This booklet is not about religion itself. It is about the use people have made of religion in the recorded past. In the next few pages we shall look at the ways in which religions have affected societies, beginning with a short summary.

Both small and large-scale religions affected human society in many ways. The gods had to be treated in the correct way: so correct beliefs (*doctrine*) and correct ceremonies (*ritual*) had to be established. Special people were needed to perform the ritual, and to set down and teach the doctrine, so *priests* and other learned men became important.

Christmas card

Religion	Origin	Founder	Area to which it spread	Main areas in 20th century	Main Divisions	Booklets with more information
Buddhism	North India in 6th century BC From Hinduism	Gautama Buddha (c.563– 483 BC)	Asia	S.E. Asia (Burma, Ceylon, Cambodia, Laos, Thailand) China & Japan	Mahayana Theravada	*Asoka and Indian Civilization* *Angkor*
Christianity	Palestine in 1st century AD From Judaism	Jesus of Nazareth (c. 4BC– c.29AD)	Africa Americas Asia Australasia Europe	Americas Australasia Europe	Orthodox Protestant Roman Catholic	*Constantine* *The Middle Ages*
Confucianism & Taoism	China in 5th BC	Confucius (551– Lao-tzu (6th century BC)	China Korea	China Korea	Many	*Traditional China*
Hinduism	North India c.1000 BC	Unknown	India S.E. Asia	India	Many	*Asoka and Indian Civilization*
Islam	Arabia in 7th century AD	Muhammad (c.570– 632 AD)	Africa Asia	Africa Middle East Central Asia South Asia South-east Asia	Sunnite Shiite	*Muhammad and the Arab Empire* *Ibn Sina*

A member of the Bundu, a women's secret society in Sierra Leone, which gave magical protection against illness

Organizations grew up to regulate religious work. Out of these things in turn grew many other ways in which religion affected life. Art, music, and architecture; law; ways of behaving; education: all have been closely connected with religion. These features are not all equally important in all religions. For example, the Roman Catholic and some other Christian Churches are highly organized, but Hindus by comparison have little religious organization.

Religious Beliefs

The beliefs of different religions vary a great deal, but in several of them the idea of one great God is most important. In the Jewish and Christian religions, only one God can be worshipped. The same is true of Islam. This belief in one God is called *monotheism.* Hindus, on the other hand, believe in many gods, although some believe that one god is greater than all the others. Hinduism, though, is a mixture of all sorts of beliefs including one view that all gods are really only different ideas of the same god.

A famous story tells how a group of blind men came across an elephant. One felt the elephant's leg and said that the elephant was like a tree trunk. Another felt its tail and said that it was like a rope. A third felt its trunk and said that it was like a snake, and so on. Obviously the men's ideas were very different. Nevertheless they were describing the same thing, and they were all partly correct. The same could be true of men's ideas about God.

For the men in the story, God is mysterious. Man has always found it difficult to explain his ideas of God, but in most religions we find the idea that God created the world and keeps it in existence. Another important and common idea is that he loves human beings, and will help and comfort them in times of trouble; but if they lead bad lives, he will punish them when they die. Ideas of life after death, and of Heaven and Hell, have been very common all over the world. Hindus and Buddhists believe in *reincarnation* (being born again). According to how good or bad a man had been in his life he would be born again as a higher or lower creature. In China, this Buddhist idea existed side by side with ancestor worship, a tradition that has been followed in many parts of the world.

Religion tries to find the purpose of life and death, and to give an explanation of the whole universe. Not all religions, however, have a belief in God. For example, Buddhism believes that it can offer practical help to men without bothering with theories about God or creation or eternal life (D4).

Religious Specialists

All religions have had religious specialists, from witch doctor to priest. Partly this was because trained men were needed to carry out rituals. In Judaism, Christianity and Islam, religious specialists have had much power because these religions are what we call *revealed* religions, that is they depend on messages given to chosen people by God. The Bible and the Koran are such messages. A message from God was so important that specially trained men were needed to understand it and to explain to others what the message meant.

Some religions, such as Hinduism, Buddhism and Confucianism, also have ancient writings which, although they are not thought to be the word of God, are still believed to be very important. Those who could read and understand them had great power over other people. Sometimes the holy books were written in languages which ordinary people could not read. The medieval European Bible was in Latin, the Hindu writings in Sanskrit and the Koran in Arabic, which non-Arab Muslims usually could not understand. In many societies the religious specialists were the only people who could read and write. The link between religion and education thus became very close. (*Education*)

Many of the historical records of different countries were kept by religious people.

Religious specialists have often held positions of great power and privilege in their societies. In India the Brahmins were the top social class or caste as it is termed in India (D5, D6). (*Asoka and Indian Civilization*) In medieval Europe

Indian sadhu, or holy man

Hinduism: Brahmin at prayer

bishops and abbots were very wealthy and powerful *(The Middle Ages)*; in Islam the *ulema* were the most respected people *(Ibn Sina)*; and in ancient Peru the priests' fields were cultivated before those of even the Emperor. (*Ancient America*) Sometimes religious leaders have used their positions in order to gain riches and power for themselves (D7).

The Organization of Religion

Any group of people who do something together become organized as the group gets bigger. The bigger a group becomes usually the more highly organized it becomes. As groups of people of similar beliefs banded together so religions became organized. As well as a special place, such as a temple or church, and special people, such as priests, religious organizations have also had *lay* members (members who were not priests). Some might work for the organization but most would be followers, with some being more

11

Medieval French religious hospital

devout than others.

In some cases the organization became very large, operating on a national or even international scale. This was the case with some branches of the Christian Church, and especially the Roman Catholic Church, whose world-wide organization is headed by the Pope. Other religions, perhaps just as widespread, were organized on a more local basis with each group — whether centered on a mosque, synagogue or temple — quite separate from the others. In these cases it was the beliefs and practices, rather than the organization, that held the religion together.

Monasteries — A refuge from the world

Some kinds of religious organizations (with their centre being an individual church or temple) are concerned with ordinary people and the place of religion in their daily lives. But throughout the centuries there have been people who wished to cut themselves off from the world and live entirely for their religion. Sometimes a man would live on his own as a *hermit*, usually very simply and in a remote place. Later, groups of religious-minded people came together and lived in *monasteries* (from a Greek word meaning 'alone'). Monasteries became known as places of peace and refuge from a harsh, dangerous, insecure and violent world, and they developed in many countries. From the tenth century in Europe they increased in numbers and importance and became highly organized. They owned and farmed large areas of land and even ran industries. *(The Middle Ages)* Monasteries became even more important in the Buddhist countries of Tibet and South-east Asia where they became a vital part of the economy and government (D8). Some Buddhists may live as monks for a time, and then return to normal life.

Although some monasteries were completely enclosed and cut off from the world, there were many others which received visitors. Indeed, many monks regarded it as their duty to care for the poor and the sick and to offer hospitality to travellers. In this way, monks established some of the first hospitals and welfare

The Book of Kells (about eighth century A.D.) is a copy of the Gospels, and is one of the finest early illuminated manuscripts

services.

They also made a great contribution to the field of knowledge and learning. Because monks had peace, quiet and a great deal of time, they were able to study, and to read and write books. Many manuscripts written in the monasteries were very beautifully produced, sometimes with richly coloured ornament known as *illumination.* Monks could often become very important as scholars and teachers.

Art, Architecture, Music and Religion

Throughout the world many of the finest buildings and greatest works of art have been inspired by religion. Sometimes, as in Africa, the paintings and carvings were objects used in acts of worship and were not meant to be works of art. Elsewhere, as in Renaissance Italy, the paintings and sculpture had religious themes but were intended to impress and adorn. Buddhist carvings and Hindu paintings are among the finest examples of Eastern art.

Often the place of worship was the only permanent building and had to be a place fit for gods or spirits. Religious architecture therefore produced the most important buildings in many societies, for example, the pyramids of Egypt; the great temples of ancient America; the cathedrals of medieval Europe; the pagodas of Burma and the temples of Japan.

Music was often used in worship, especially by Jews and Christians, and European classical music owes much to the work of the Church and the inspiration of religion. The great composer Johann Sebastian Bach (1685–1750) began his career as a church organist, and the famous *Messiah* by George Frederick Handel (1685–1759) is about Jesus.

Religion and Law

As well as links between religion and education or art there has also been a close relationship between religion and law. Confucianism is really nothing more than a collection of laws or rules about behaviour. Many African societies believed that God had established their laws. This belief has been fairly common throughout history. The Babylonian king Hammurabi (1792-1750 B.C.) (*Ancient Near East*) whose collection of laws was one of the most important in the ancient world, claimed to have received them from Shamash the sun god (D9).

In some societies the ruler himself was seen as a sort of god (D10), and because of this the laws he made were like laws from God. This was true of the kings of ancient Egypt and the Inca emperors who were said to have been descended from the sun god. (*The Ancient Near East; Ancient America*) In Japan, right up to the end of the Second World War in 1945, the Emperor was thought to be directly descended from the sun goddess, Amaterasu. (*Japan's Modernization*)

In Judaism can be seen the mixture of religion, law and morality. The Jews call the first

Hindu goddess Durga, or Kali

five books of the Bible the *Torah* (law). The Torah contains details of sacrifices and festivals, but it also includes rules of morality like the Ten Commandments, believed to have been received direct from God by Moses, and the famous saying, 'love your neighbour as yourself', which Jesus was to repeat later.

The Potala in Lhasa, home of the Dalai Lama

The Torah also contains laws for running the whole of society. Jewish communities have often formed parts of much larger Christian or Muslim societies, yet they have nearly always chosen to run their own communities according to laws based on the Torah. This has been an important factor in holding their society together.

Similarly, Muslims have based their laws on the Koran and the sayings of their prophet Mohammed. These came to form the *Sharia*, the laws which have governed Muslim countries until the last two hundred years, and which still form the basis of family law in most Muslim countries. (*Ibn Sina*) This is an example of how, through its associations with law, religion could be a source of great continuity and stability. There was, however, a danger of getting stuck in the past, and this became a difficulty in Muslim countries from the eighteenth century as they attempted to modernize. As economic, political and social conditions changed, laws became out of date, but there was much opposition to changing what were thought of as God's laws. (*Ataturk*) Again, in China, the old Confucian system which stressed the importance of studying the Chinese Classics made reform of education more difficult. (*Chinese Revolution; Mao Tse-tung*)

RELIGION AND POLITICS

Religion and Government

Throughout history religion and government have been closely intertwined. Kings and other rulers had to take account of the views of religious organizations. The importance in society of religious specialists has already been mentioned. Because of their education and knowledge of law, they often served kings and princes as administrators. For example, in England there was a long line of Lord Chancellors who were priests. The most famous of these was probably Thomas Becket. Sometimes a religious leader was a prince in his own right – e.g., the Pope, with lands and armies of his own like any other ruler. The Vatican City is a reminder of the Papal States which were governed by the Popes of Rome from 756 to 1870 and which included large parts of Italy. Another example is Tibet which, until 1959, was ruled by the chief monk, the Dalai Lama. He lived in an enormous palace in the capital city of Lhasa.

Political Ideas

Religious ideas have had important political effects. Indeed in Islam there was no distinction between religious and political ideas. Muslims divided the world into two parts – the land of Islam and the land of war. It was the duty of Muslims to wage war (*jihad*) in order to bring the land of war under Muslim rule. Religious ideas were also used to teach people to respect and obey their rulers. The stability of the Chinese Empire over many centuries owed much to the teachings of Confucius which were officially recognized by the rulers of China. The Chinese Emperor (like the kings of medieval Europe) was thought to rule by Divine Right (D11); the Chinese called it the Mandate of Heaven. (*Traditional China*) Christianity also taught obedience. St Paul, in his letter to the Christians at Rome, said 'Let every person be subject to the governing authorities. For there is no authority except from God, and those that exist have been instituted by God.' Martin Luther (1483-1546) referred to St Paul with approval, and said, 'Rebellion can never be right, however just the cause'. (*Luther, Erasmus and Loyola*) If a ruler were unjust, God would punish him: it was not for men to do so.

Because official religion usually taught people to obey their rulers and support the structure of society, those who wanted a change were often forced to propose a change of religious ideas as well. Rebellion came to be the same as *heresy* (beliefs that religious leaders considered to be wrong and dangerous). One reason why most religions have attacked heretics so fiercely is because they threatened not only the religion but also the government and the way society was run.

Ideas of Equality

Religious ideas of the equality of men before God, and of the brotherhood of all men, have sometimes led people to adopt political views very like those of modern communists (D12, 13). Hung Hsui-ch'uan, leader of the Taiping rebellion in nineteenth-century China, thought that he was the brother of Jesus Christ, and was going to overthrow the Emperor and establish a 'Heavenly Kingdom of Great Peace'. (*The Chinese Revolution*) In seventeenth-century England there were many extremist religious groups. One such group was called the 'levellers' because they wanted to rid society of the enormous inequalities between rich and poor (D14). In India a variety of protest movements occurred from the seventeenth century onwards whose main aim was to abolish the caste (class) system. Buddhism

Ely Place, a small part of London ruled by the Church

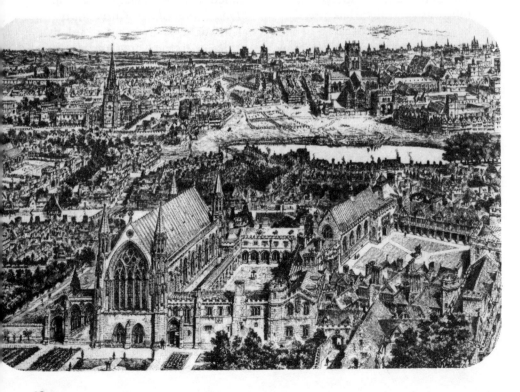

and Islam spread in India partly because people turned to them from Hinduism in order to escape from the poor position in which they had been placed by the caste system.

TOLERANCE

Religious disagreements have often been harsh, especially in Christianity and Islam. The Inquisition (a Catholic church court set up in the Middle Ages) set out to find heretics and witches. Suspects were questioned and sometimes tortured to make them confess their sins and ask God's forgiveness. Those who asked for forgiveness were punished by the Inquisition; those who refused were *excommunicated* (forced to leave the Church) and given to the State to be executed, sometimes by being burnt alive (D15). With the Reformation the attempt to keep western Christendom united broke down. (*Luther, Erasmus and Loyola*) For more than a hundred years European states fought each other, partly about religion, and most refused to allow their subjects to hold differing religious views. In the eighteenth century the wars of religion in Europe gave way to greater tolerance in religion. (*The Enlightenment*)

There have also been wars between religions. Islam and Christianity were at war for most of their history. In 1096 the Christian crusaders began the series of wars known as the Crusades to try to recover Palestine, which they regarded as the Holy Land, from the Muslims and to keep it. From the seventh to the seventeenth centuries Muslim rulers struggled to conquer Europe. In India there was often war between Muslims and Hindus and as late as 1947 the country was divided on religious lines amid scenes of great violence. (*Gandhi*) Christians have also persecuted Jews for much of history. Jews also suffered heavily under the Nazis in Germany who, between 1942 and 1945, killed an estimated six million Jews. (*Hitler's Reich*)

Other religions existed together happily so that a person could even belong to more than one of them at the same time. In Japan people worshipped sometimes at a Buddhist temple and sometimes at a Shinto shrine, or were married at one and buried at the other. At times in China, a scholar might wear Buddhist robes and a Confucian hat, and carry a Taoist staff, to show his belief that the three religions were all part of the same truth.

Some religions have thought that it was important to try to convert people (D16). Christian churches sent missionaries all over the world, especially in the nineteenth century, and these missionaries were important in spreading education and medical care (D17). Buddhist monks also acted as missionaries as they travelled through Asia. Learned Muslims converted people to Islam in Bengal, South-east Asia, and Africa. By contrast, China, although it imported Buddhism, did not export Confucianism and Taoism except to Japan and Vietnam. Similarly, Hinduism has made little impact outside India.

Trinity College, Dublin, 1850, the cultural centre of Protestant rule in Ireland

except in South-east Asia.

Sometimes attempts have been made to bring opposing religions together. For example, by the fifteenth century a movement had developed in northern India to build a bridge between Hinduism and Islam. The poet Kabir supported this movement and his ideas influenced Nanak (1469–1538), a religious reformer from the Punjab, who organized his followers into a community under himself as *Guru* (teacher). Yet although they themselves accepted parts of both Hinduism and Islam, they could not bring the two religions together. Instead they created a new religion; the religion of the Sikhs (D18).

The ideas of toleration inspired by Kabir made a great impression on the Muslim emperor Akbar, who set a notable example by trying to develop understanding between different faiths. (*Akbar and the Mughal Empire*) This is an aim that many people try to achieve in the twentieth century.

Religion and Politics in Modern Times

In the last few hundred years religion has affected politics in many ways. In certain cases it has become linked with nationalism (D19). (*Nationalism*) For example, when the old rulers of Japan were overthrown in 1868 and the Emperor was restored to power, the old Shinto religion was encouraged by the new rulers. It helped both to strengthen the position of the Emperor and to foster the spirit of Japanese nationalism. (*Japan's Modernization*)

Religious beliefs have often been opposed to social and political changes in modern times, for example to changes in the laws on divorce and to new forms of education. However, religious beliefs have sometimes helped in the process of modernization. During the eighteenth century in Arabia a religious movement, the Wahhabi Movement, developed with the aim of abolishing new ideas in the Muslim world and returning to original Islam. Gradually it became a political movement which helped to turn warlike

Shinto shrine in Japan

nomadic tribes into peaceful farmers and also to build the modern state of Saudi Arabia.

This example shows that while religious movements may appear to reject the modern world, they are more concerned with stopping changes in the way people behave in their personal lives. They are usually willing to accept much wider changes such as the increase in the power of the state, and industrialization and urbanization. In Egypt during the 1930s and 1940s there was a strong religious political movement called the Muslim Brotherhood. The Brothers called for Egyptians to turn their backs on European ideas and to return to Islam. In practice they wanted to take those European ideas which would make Egypt strong and throw out things like modern dance halls and alcohol (D20).

SECULARISM

As we have seen, religion has had great influence throughout history in such varied fields as education, art, politics and morality, and has also been of considerable help to man in interpreting his place in the world and the universe. In the nineteenth and twentieth centuries religion was challenged by *Secularism*, the idea that man is 'growing up' and no longer needs religion. Secular thinkers believe that the gods, or God, do not really exist but that man invented them as a source of help to explain things about the universe which he did not understand.

Now that man knows much more about himself, the secularists say,

he can have the courage to believe in himself, in humanity, and so to be a *Humanist* (D21).

Secularism has had two sources. The first lies in the disappearance of some of the *functions* of religion, that is the things it does. As we have seen, religion in human history has not just been a question of personal belief; it has also been the basis of law, government and education. In the past two hundred years these last aspects of religion have faded: the state has made new laws to replace the old religious laws; the state has become the main provider of education; and the state no longer depends upon religion to justify its own power. (*The Growth of the State*) So many of the reasons why religion flourished in the past have now gone.

The second source of secularism is the decline of personal belief. Science seems to have shown that many of the explanations of the universe which religion offered were wrong. (*Darwin*) Many people therefore reject religion. Also many people feel more secure than people did centuries ago and therefore do not want the comfort which religion gave to people in the past. (*Health and Wealth*) Some people resent the way religious rules interfere with their lives.

But no one has yet explained the purpose of life, if it has one, and for many people religion still offers an answer to this great question and still provides rules to help them live their lives. Indeed religions share important values both with each other and with humanism (D22).

DOCUMENT 1

HYMN TO THE SUN-GOD   *This example is taken from ancient Egypt, about 1350 B.C. The god's name is Re, and the King is called his son.*

Beautiful in thine appearing in the horizon of heaven, thou living sun, the first who lived.
Thou riseth in the eastern horizon, and Thou fillest every land with thy beauty.
Thou art beautiful and great and glisteneth, and art high above every land;
Thy rays, they compass the lands, so far as all that thou hast created.
Thou art Re, and thou reachest unto their end and subduest them for thy dear Son.
Though thou art far away, yet are thy rays upon earth;
Thou art before their face — thy going.

DOCUMENT 2

A CHINESE MYTH OF THE CREATION OF THE WORLD

At the outset the Universe was an egg. One day the egg split open. The top half became the sky and the bottom half the earth. Pan-ku, who emerged from the broken egg, grew three metres taller every day, just as the sky became three metres higher and the earth three metres thicker. After eighteen thousand years Pan-ku died. Then, like the original egg, he split into a number of parts. His head formed the sun and moon, his blood the rivers and seas, his hair the forests, his sweat the rain, his breath the wind, his voice thunder, and, last of all, his fleas became the ancestors of mankind.

DOCUMENT 3

ALCHEMY   *A second-century Chinese alchemist tries out an elixir; a description taken from a fourth-century document*

Wei Po-Yang passed into the mountains to prepare magical elixirs. With him went three disciples. When the elixir was achieved he decided to make a trial of them. 'The gold elixir is now made', he said, 'but it ought first to be tested. Let us give it to this white dog.'
So Wei Po-Yang fed it to the dog, and the dog immediately fell down dead. Turning to the disciples he said: 'I fear the elixir was not perfected. As it has killed the dog it would seem that we have not grasped the full theory of spiritual power. If we take it now I am afraid that we shall go the same way as the animal. What do you think we should do?' The

disciples, perplexed, replied by another question: 'Would you, Sir, dare to take it yourself?' He answered: 'I abandoned worldly ways and forsook family and friends to enter into the mountains; I should be ashamed to return without having found the path of the Holy Immortals. To die of the elixir would be no worse than living without it. I must take it.' And he did, whereupon no sooner was it in his mouth than he fell dead . . . .

On seeing this one of the disciples said: 'Our teacher was no ordinary person; what he has done he did with intention', so he too swallowed the elixir and died. Then the other two said to one another: 'Those who prepare elixirs do so to gain immortal life. But now this elixir has brought death. It would be better not to take it, and live in the world a few more decades instead.' So together they left the mountains, intending to get coffins and other things for the burial of their teacher and fellow-disciple.

After they had gone Wei Po-Yang revived, and so did the disciple, and so did the white dog, and they all went away further into the mountains (to tread the path of the immortals). On the way they met a wood-cutter by whom the Master sent a letter to the two disciples thanking them for their kindness. But when they read it their hearts were filled with grief and regret.

DOCUMENT 4

THE SAYINGS OF THE BUDDHA: *HAPPINESS*

We live happily indeed, not hating those who hate us. Among men who hate us we live free from hatred. We live happily, free from sickness among the sick.

We live happily free from greed among the greedy.

We live happily though we call nothing our own. We shall be like the bright gods, feeding on happiness.

Victory breeds hatred for the defeated are unhappy. The contented man who has given up victory and defeat is happy.

There is no fire like passion; nothing so futile as hatred; no pain like those of the body; no happiness greater than rest.

Hunger is the worst disease; the parts of the body the worst evil. If one truly understands this one has reached Nirvana, the highest happiness.

Health is the greatest gift; to be content the best of riches; trust is the best of relationships; Nirvana the highest happiness.

He who has discovered how sweet it is to be alone and at peace is free from fear and sin and lives in the comfort of the law.

DOCUMENT 5

BRAHMINS   *LAWS OF MANU — The most authoritative Hindu law-book (200 B.C.–A.D. 200). It emphasizes the powers and privileges of the priests.*

Of all creatures the animate are said to be the best, of animate beings those who live on their wits, of those who live on their wits, men, and among men Brahmins are the best . . . . When a Brahmin is born he is born superior to the whole earth, he is the lord of all creatures, and he has to guard the treasury of *dharma* [religion and its laws]. Everything that exists throughout the world is the private property of the Brahmin. By the high excellence of his birth he is entitled to everything. What he enjoys, what he wears, and what he gives away are his own private property, and it is through the mercy of the Brahmin that others enjoy anything at all.

DOCUMENT 6

BRAHMINS   *MARCO POLO — The thirteenth-century Italian traveller*

I assure you that these Brahmins are among the best traders in the world and the most reliable. They would not tell a lie for anything in the world and do not utter a word that is not true. They eat no meat and drink no wine. They live very virtuous lives according to their usage. They take nothing that belongs to another. They would never kill a living creature or do any act that they believe to be sinful.

DOCUMENT 7

CORRUPT CLERGYMEN   *JOHN OF SALISBURY — Writing in the Middle Ages about Christian priests*

They love bribes; they are revengeful and prone to injury. They rejoice in calumny [defamation/slander], eat and drink the sins of the people, and live on robbery . . . . Their high office makes it their duty to keep God's Law, yet they keep it not.

DOCUMENT 8

MONASTERIES IN TIBET   *F. SPENCER CHAPMAN — A British traveller who visited Tibet in 1936-37*

As we were given the opportunity of visiting the great monasteries of Lhasa we learnt a little of the traditions and way of life of these immense organizations which resolutely turn their backs on progress, realizing that their very existence depends on the exclusion of outside influence and enlightenment.

Practically half the revenue of the State is devoted to the upkeep of the monasteries either in the form of grants of land or in gifts of barley, butter and tea. Another source of income is gifts from regular worshippers and pilgrims. Fees are also paid on the innumerable occasions when monks have to be called in, or special prayers offered at the monasteries. The monks are not slow to exploit the power that is given to them by the superstitious and credulous Tibetan. In a thousand ways the co-operation of the 'lama' is needed by the layman to avoid perdition [hell] and to give him the highest possible chance of a successful rebirth. It is not surprising that the monasteries are the most wealthy and powerful institutions in Tibet.

Tibet is a poor country and the land will only support a certain number of people. If the working families have more children than they can afford to keep, the surplus are sent to the neighbouring monastery or nunnery, where they are brought up at the expense of the State. More than one sixth of the male population of Tibet are monks.

DOCUMENT 9

THE CODE OF HAMMURABI   *Words of warning to rulers who fail to uphold these laws (18th century B.C.)*

Hammurabi, the king of righteousness, whom Shamash has endowed with justice, am I. My words are weighty; my deeds are unrivalled . . . .

If that man does not pay attention to my words which I have written upon my monument, does not alter my statutes, then will Shamash prolong that man's reign, as he has mine, who am king of righteousness, that he may rule his people in righteousness.

If that man does not pay attention to my words which I have written upon my monument; if he forgets my curse and does not fear the curse of god; if he abolishes the judgments which I have formulated, overrules my words, alters my statutes, effaces my name written thereon and writes his own name . . . as for that man, be he king or lord, or priest-king or commoner, whoever he may be, may the great god, the father of the gods, who has ordained my reign, take from him the glory of his sovereignty, may he break his sceptre and curse his fate!

DOCUMENT 10

ASSYRIAN PROVERB   *(about 670 B.C.)*

Man is but the shadow of a god, a slave is the shadow of a man; but the King is the very image of a god.

DOCUMENT 11

DIVINE RIGHT OF KINGS   *IN SHAKESPEARE'S PLAY – King Richard the Second claims that kings hold their power from God*

Not all the water in the rough rude sea
Can wash the balm off from an anointed king;
The breath of worldly men cannot depose
The deputy elected by the Lord.

DOCUMENT 12

A COMMUNIST SERMON   *JOHN BALL – Preaching during the English Peasants' Revolt of 1381*

And if we are all descended from one father and one mother, Adam and Eve, how can the lords say or prove that they are more lords than we are – save that they make us dig and till the ground so that they can squander what we produce? They are clad in velvet and satin, set off with squirrel fur, while we are dressed in poor cloth. They have wines and spices and fine bread, and we have only rye and spoilt flour and straw, and only water to drink. They have beautiful residences and manors, while we have the trouble and the work, always in the fields under rain and snow. But it is from us and our labour that everything comes with which they maintain their pomp . . . . Good folk, things cannot go well in England nor ever shall until all things are in common and there is neither villein nor noble, but all of us are of one condition.

DOCUMENT 13

A HERESY IN ISLAM   *The following extract from an Arabic manuscript tells how religion was used to form a communist society in Iraq during the ninth century*

When this was completed he imposed on them the duty of union. This meant that they assembled their possessions in one place and held them in common, no man enjoying any advantage over his friend because of any property which he owned. He read them God's words and told them that they had no need of possessions because the earth in its entirety would be theirs and no one else's. In every village the missionaries chose and appointed a man whom they trusted to collect all the possessions of the villagers, by way of cattle, sheep and goats, jewellery and other things; he then clothed the naked and supplied their needs so that no poor man remained among them.

Every man worked diligently at his trade; the woman brought him what she earned by weaving and the child brought his wages for scaring away birds. No one owned anything but his sword and his arms. When all this was established he ordered the missionaries to assemble all the women on a certain night to mix with the men. This, he said, was true love and union between them. When he was sure of their obedience be began to lead them astray. He made them cast off the Holy Law. He removed all restraints from them concerning property and sexuality and freed them from fasting, prayer and the commandments. He taught them that the knowledge of the Master of Truth, for whom he preached, dispensed them from everything, and that they need have no fear of sin or punishment.

DOCUMENT 14

GOD MADE THE WORLD FOR EVERYONE   *GERARD WINSTANLEY — An English radical of the seventeenth century, who believed that social and economic inequality was contrary to God's will. His ideas were similar to those of the Levellers, but if anything, more extreme*

In the beginning of time the great Creator, Reason, made the earth to be a common treasury, to preserve beasts, birds, fishes and man, the lord that was to govern this creation . . . . Not one word was spoken in the beginning that one branch of mankind should rule over another . . . . But selfish imaginations did set up one man to teach and rule over another. And thereby man was brought into bondage, and became a greater slave to such of his own kind than the beasts of the field were to him. And hereupon the earth was hedged into enclosures by the teachers and rulers, and the others were made slaves. And that earth that is within this creation made a common storehouse for all, is bought and sold and kept in the hands of a few, whereby the great Creator is mightily dishonoured, as if he were a respecter of persons, delighting in the comfortable liveli-hood of some, and rejoicing in the miserable poverty and straits of others. From the beginning it was not so.

DOCUMENT 15

A VICTIM OF PERSECUTION   *A letter of 24 July 1628 from the Mayor of Bamberg, in Germany, to his daughter*

Innocent have I come to prison, innocent have I been tortured, innocent must I die. For whoever comes into the witch prison must become a witch or be tortured until he invents something out of his head . . . . I will tell you how it has gone with me . . . . And then came — God in highest heaven have mercy — the executioner, and put the thumbscrews on me, so that the blood ran out of the nails and everywhere, so that for four weeks I could not use my hands as you can see from the writing . . . . Thereafter they first stripped me, bound my hands behind me, and drew me up in the torture; (by means of a rope attached to the hands tied behind the back, and carried over a pulley on the ceiling.) Then I thought Heaven and Earth were at an end; eight times did they draw me up and let me fall again, so that I suffered terrible agony. The executioner said, 'Sir, I beg you for God's sake confess something, whether it be true or not, for you cannot endure the torture which you will be put to . . . .'

DOCUMENT 18

SIKHISM   *ARJUN – The fifth Guru of the Sikhs (1563-1606)*

> I have broken with the Hindu and the Muslim,
> I will not worship with the Hindu, nor like the Muslim go to Mecca.
> I shall serve Him and no other.
> I will not pray to idols nor say the Muslim prayer.
> I shall put my heart at the feet of the one Supreme Being,
> For we are neither Hindus nor Musulmans.

DOCUMENT 16

MISSIONARIES SPREAD CHRISTIANITY   *An edict of Peter the Great of Russia, 17 June 1700. Peter also hoped to strengthen Russian political control over Siberia*

For the strengthening of the Orthodox Christian faith and for the proclamation of the Christian faith among the idolatrous peoples; also in order to bring the tributary peoples of Siberia to Christian faith and holy baptisms, the Metropolitan [bishop] of Kiev should seek out a virtuous and learned man of good and blameless life to be Metropolitan of Tobolsk and with God's help gradually bring those peoples in Siberia and China who live in the blindness of idolatry, and generally in ignorance, to the knowledge, the service and the worship of the true and living God.

DOCUMENT 17

MISSIONARIES AND EDUCATION   *A letter from a London Missionary Society missionary in Bengal, 1825*

Though the Scriptures are not used in the Government Schools, we improve every opportunity of imparting religious knowledge to the children. We generally cause them to leave their school room and collecting them under some shady trees examine them regarding their progress in learning, and as every first principle which they learn in geography or astronomy contradicts the statements which they have heard from their Shastres [he means their Hindu religious teachers] on these subjects, an extensive field for observation and enquiry is at once opened before them. Their friends and others soon collect around us and on these occasions we sometimes have our largest congregations and many useful subjects are discussed.

DOCUMENT 19

RELIGION, NATIONALISM AND MODERNIZATION   *AUROBINDO GHOSE — An Indian philosopher, speaking about Hinduism in 1908*

What is the Hindu religion? It is the Hindu religion only because the Hindu nation has kept it, because in this peninsula it grew up in the seclusion of the sea and the Himalayas, because in this sacred and ancient land it was given as a charge to the Aryan race to preserve through the ages. But it does not belong peculiarly and forever to a bounded part of the world. That which we call the Hindu religion is really the eternal religion, because it is the universal religion which embraces all others. This is the one religion that can triumph over materialism by including and anticipating the discoveries of science and the speculations of philosophy. I spoke once and said that this movement is not a political movement and that nationalism is not politics but a religion, a creed, a faith. I say it again today but I put it another way. I say that it is (Hinduism) which for us is nationalism.

DOCUMENT 20

RELIGION AND THE STATE   *A statement by the leader of the Muslim Brotherhood, one of the largest and most powerful political parties in Egypt before 1952*

We believe the provisions of Islam and its teachings are all inclusive, encompassing the affairs of people in this world and the hereafter. And those who think that these teachings are concerned only with the spiritual or ritualistic aspects are mistaken in this belief because Islam is a faith and a ritual, a nation and a nationality, a religion and a state, spirit and deed, holy text and sword.

DOCUMENT 21

RELIGION GIVES WAY TO HUMANISM   *WINWOOD READE — Author of* The Martyrdom of Man, *published first in 1872. In this history of the world Reade looks forward to a time when man has outgrown religion and lives by humanist rules*

All attempts to define the Creator bring us only to ridiculous conclusions. We are to infer that Man is not made in the image of his Maker, and that Man can no more understand his Maker than the beetles and the

worms can understand him. As men in the Days of Ignorance
endeavoured to discover perpetual motion and the philosopher's stone,
so now they endeavour to define God. But in time also they will learn
that the nature of the Deity is beyond the powers of the human intellect
to solve. The universe is anonymous. . . .

There is only one Man upon the earth; what we call men are not
individuals but components; what we call death is merely the bursting of
a cell; wars and epidemics are merely inflammatory phenomena . . . .
There is no such thing as a ghost or a soul. If we take the life of a single
atom, that is to say of a single man, or if we look only at a single group,
all appears to be cruelty and confusion; but when we survey mankind as
one, we find it becoming more and more noble, more and more divine,
slowly ripening towards perfection. . . .

The following facts result from our investigations: Supernatural Christianity is false. God-worship is idolatry. Prayer is useless. The soul is not
immortal. There are no rewards and there are no punishments in a future
state.

DOCUMENT 22

LOVE AS A BASIC HUMAN VALUE

Babylonian tablet, before 700 B.C.
Unto your opponent do no evil;
Your evildoer recompense with good;
Unto your enemy let justice be done.

Confucius, 551-479 B.C.
Do not do to others what you would not desire yourself.

Dhammapada, Buddhist scripture, c.250 B.C.
Hate is not conquered by hate: hate is conquered by love. This is a law
eternal. . . .
Overcome anger by peacefulness; overcome evil by good. Overcome the
man by generosity; and the man who lies by truth.

Jesus, according to the Gospel of Matthew
You have learned that they were told, 'Love your neighbour, hate your
enemy'.
But what I tell you is this: 'Love your enemies and pray for your
persecutors'.

Basavanna, twelfth-century Hindu saint
Where is religion without loving-kindness?

Hillel, Jewish teacher, 50 B.C.–A.D.25

Whatever is hateful unto thee, do it not unto thy fellow.

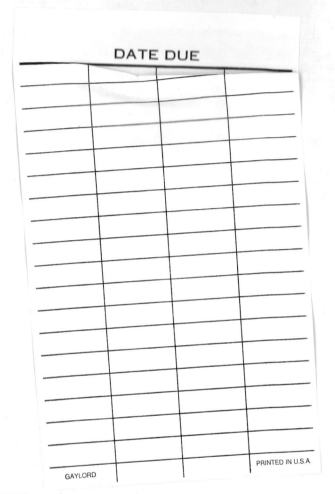

ACKNOWLEDGEMENTS

Illustrations

The Mansell Collection pages 3, 13, 15; Mary Evans Picture Library page 11; Radio Times Hulton Picture Library pages 4, 5, 7, 8, 10, 12, 16, 18, 20, 21.

Documents

D1 *The Concept of Deity*, E. O. Jones, Hutchinson; D2, *The Early Civilization of China*, A. Cotterell, Weidenfeld & Nicolson; D3, *Science and Civilization in China*, J. Needham, Cambridge Univeristy Press; D8, *Lhasa, the Holy City*, Spencer Chapman, Chatto & Windus.